BLUE PETER SPECIAL ASSIGNMENT
Hong Kong and Malta

From   Mrs kare

1980

BLUE PETER SPECIAL ASSIGNMENT

Hong Kong and Malta

EDWARD BARNES and DOROTHY SMITH

With full colour photographs
and with line drawings by Robert Broomfield

BRITISH BROADCASTING CORPORATION

Published by the British Broadcasting Corporation,
35 Marylebone High Street, London W1M 4AA

ISBN 0 563 12834 8
First published 1975

The photographs for this volume are by
Ray Cranbourne (Hong Kong) and Victor Camilleri (Malta)

Printed in England
by Tinling (1973) Limited
(a member of the Oxley Printing Group)

Blue Peter Special Assignment

HONG KONG:	Film Cameraman	Ken Westbury B.S.C.
	Sound Recordist	John Gatland
	Director	Edward Barnes
MALTA:	Film Cameraman	Yousuf Aziz
	Sound Recordist	John Hore
	Director	Harry Cowdy
	Historical Research by	Dorothy Smith
	Research Assistant	Jane Tarleton
	Producer	Edward Barnes

Hello there!

This year's Blue Peter Special Assignments are about islands.

There's something romantic about the very word! It's an adventure to visit an island—and islands like to be visited. Islanders are proud individual people; they may welcome you to their shore, but you will always remain someone from the mainland. The Governor of the Isle of Wight, Earl Mountbatten of Burma, told me: "If you're not an islander, you're an overner. You may be a very pretty overner, but you're an overner for all that!"

These books are about five islands I've visited, from faraway exotic Hong Kong to the remote and beautiful Isle of Skye. They were all totally different from each other, yet they all had one thing in common; the islanders all believed *they* lived somewhere that was very special indeed.

Valerie Singleton

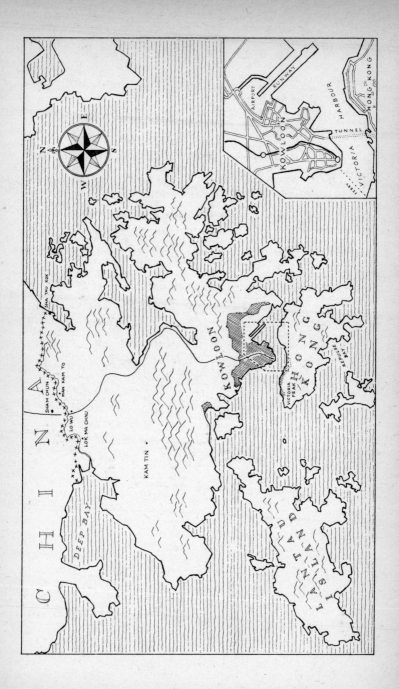

HONG KONG

The Hairiest Landing in the World

"Ladies and gentlemen, this is the Captain speaking. We shall shortly be landing at Hong Kong. We shall be flying rather close to the mountains, and to some of the buildings, just before we land. Please don't be alarmed—I can assure you that we have done it before!"

The V.C.10 skimmed between two skyscrapers, and I could actually see the Chinese faces of children playing basketball in the school below.

"Hong Kong—Ascot double two five zero—established inbound"—the Captain radioed to Hong Kong Control Tower.

"Double two five zero—this is Hong Kong—clear to land," a voice crackled back over the R.T.

Those clipped matter-of-fact words signalled our final approach to the airport that even experienced pilots call "the hairiest landing in the world"!

I was fortunate—I was flying with the RAF Strike Command, who can boast that they are the only major international airline that has never had a fatal accident, so I sat with my fingers crossed, hoping their luck held out.

Hong Kong isn't just a single island; there are two hundred and thirty-six islands altogether. Some are uninhabited, others support little fishing communities, but one is a highly sophisticated city.

The twin towns of Hong Kong and Kowloon, which face each other across the harbour, are built on the side of a mountain range which sweeps right down to the sea. The only way in for the planes is between the mountains and the skyscrapers, and the only place for the runway is in the sea.

"85%," said the Captain to the engineers as our starboard wing lifted over a tower block.

"80%"—we were almost down—

"Idle power—spoilers—full reverse."

As the deafening reassuring roar of the engines in reverse thrust slowed us down, and we began to turn at the end of the runway, I caught a glimpse of a Chinese junk in full red sail cutting through the little sampans in the harbour. Then the aircraft taxied slowly back towards the towering skyscrapers of downtown Kowloon.

"Lee Gardens Hotel, please," I said to the taxi-driver outside the airport.

He turned and smiled, showing a row of gold teeth. "Hong Kong side—cost you ten dollars—go through tunnel."

"O.K." I said, and we drove off, past the high-rise flats with poles of multi-coloured material poking out of every window. At first they seemed like flags put out to welcome a visiting V.I.P., until I looked a little closer and realised that they were shirts and bras and pants; everyday is wash-day for the Chinese, and the poles show how clever they are at adapting an old custom to a new style of living.

Skyscrapers reared up everywhere, and where there *was* a space, spiders' webs of flimsy bamboo scaffolding signalled the arrival of yet another tower of concrete.

The road signs looked oddly old-fashioned in such a modern city. We've got used to international ones in Britain, but here you still see the old signs—like *Slow —Major Road Ahead*—except that underneath the Chinese characters are written in translation. Every public notice and most of the advertisements in Hong

Kong are in Chinese and English, and the people speak Cantonese, which is the south China version of the Chinese language.

Kowloon, where I had arrived, is British territory stuck on to mainland China. Hong Kong island, where I was heading, is a densely populated off-shore island, separated from the mainland by less than one kilometre of water. A ferry plies backwards and forwards across the harbour every few minutes, from 6 am until 2 am the next day, and if you miss that you can always hire a walla-walla, the Cantonese name for a water-taxi. As I had all my luggage with me, I wasn't going to do either: I was going through the new tunnel. It was only finished in September of 1973; before that *everyone* took the ferry. It costs ten Hong Kong dollars every time you go through as the taxi drivers charge you for the return journey as well.

My driver slowed down to pass his money to the toll guard and we plunged underground. In two minutes we were on the island.

Victoria Peak, the mountain where the smart British residents first built their houses, rose up in the centre, and disappeared into the mist. Clinging to the sides, and sweeping down to the harbour were thousands of skyscrapers, including the second tallest in Asia. The tallest is in Tokyo, but Hong Kong has already started on another, which will be even higher.

The Founding of Hong Kong

Queen Victoria's Foreign Secretary, Lord Palmerston, said in 1841: "Hong Kong is a barren rock, with scarcely a house upon it."

In those days it was more or less that, which must have eased his conscience when he acquired the island in the name of the Queen a year later. Hong Kong became a British possession.

One hundred and thirty-three years ago the Union Jack was run up on Flagstaff House, the residence of the Commander of the British Forces, Hong Kong, and it is still flying there today.

Hong Kong was vitally important for the British. Their Empire was expanding, Free Trade was booming, and they urgently needed a base for commerce with China. For centuries wealthy Europeans had been fascinated by China, and ready to pay high prices for its jade, its ivory, its silk and its tea. Rich profits were waiting for merchants ready to take risks, but trade was impossible, because there was nothing the Chinese wanted in exchange.

The Emperor of China in his palace in Peking declared blandly: "The Heavenly Kingdom needs nothing the Red Barbarians have to offer."

They made a few grudging and reluctant concessions. European merchants were allowed into only one Chinese city—Canton, on the mouth of the Pearl River, just seventy-six miles from Hong Kong. In Canton the merchants were fenced in with regulations, forbidden to enter the town, or trade directly with its citizens. A handful of Chinese merchants controlled all their deals, and they were ordered to squeeze the foreigners as much as possible, and send the Emperor a share of the profits.

The British longed to deal with the Chinese themselves, for they found these conditions intolerable.

They appointed Lord Macartney as Ambassador to

lead a special mission to ask the Emperor for better terms. In 1795 his ships lay off the China coast.

"I shut my eyes," he said tactfully, "to the banners they fixed to our masts, declaring 'The King of the Barbarians sends tribute to the Emperor of China'!"

Mandarins from the Imperial Court waited for him on shore, and explained with great politeness the traditional ceremonies required for anyone being received by the Emperor.

The great difficulty was the kow-tow—the acknowledgement that the Emperor was a god, the Son of Heaven. Everyone entering his presence had to kneel on both knees, and strike the ground with his forehead nine times.

Lord Macartney explained politely but very firmly that the ceremonies of his country were different, but he would be proud to greet the Emperor in the same way he would greet his own king, in England. At long last this was agreed, and a day for the audience arranged.

To placate the Chinese, Lord Macartney dressed in the grandest style, in a velvet coat with the mantle of the Order of the Bath. His assistant, who was a Doctor of Laws of Oxford University, wore his scarlet degree hood.

The Emperor came in procession, with banners and standards. Seated on a palanquin carried by sixteen bearers, he advanced to meet the ambassadors. They all moved to an open pavilion prepared for them, where they exchanged gifts and partook of a most sumptuous banquet.

For five hours an entertainment was presented before them, of wrestlers, jugglers, singers and dancers.

Lord Macartney wrote in his diary: "Thus I have

Chinese Emperor

seen King Solomon in all his glory," but the outcome of the mission was very disappointing.

No concessions were granted, the policy of squeeze and harassment continued, and fifty years later the resentment between Britain and China exploded into war.

Hong Kong island was taken over by the British, and merchants and military moved in.

The new Crown Colony prospered, and trade flourished, as ships from all over the world sailed in.

The Fragrant Harbour and the Water People

Hong Kong is Chinese for "Fragrant Harbour", and the Chinese were using the harbour long before the British arrived.

The original inhabitants of Hong Kong were fishermen and their families who lived on boats in little typhoon shelters tucked away in corners of the great harbour. They were called the Tanka people which means Egg people, because they paid their taxes in eggs as they never had any cash. The Tankas were fiercely independent and despised the land so much that a man could be born on one of the little houseboats and live his whole life afloat until a coffin boat came to take him away to be buried in the earth he had always spurned.

The Water People still live in great floating villages in Hong Kong harbour although today they often go ashore. Most of the children are born in hospitals on land, and many of them go to schools on shore as well: yet still there is no need that is not catered for in the floating village.

Helen Tang, our Blue Peter interpreter, and I, hired a taxi at the quayside, because we were going to visit a family who lived in a sampan in the middle of the anchorage.

Our taxi was a tiny boat powered by a little brown-faced old lady, who could have been any age, but there was nothing frail about her. She made a keen bargain over the fare, and paddled us through the lines of boats with amazing vigour.

When I say these people do *everything* on the water, I mean it. At one moment on our journey our taxi-driver produced a chamber pot from a little cupboard under the stern, spent a penny and emptied it over the side, without so much as a by your leave!

That sequence, I may say, is *not* in the film!

We passed floating grocers' shops, floating sweet shops, floating ice-cream men, and floating restaurants

16

which brought food to your door, or, if you felt a bit hungry, would sell you a bowl of piping hot noodle soup as you rowed across the harbour. "A sort of Chinese take-away", cameraman Ken Westbury called it.

Almost every sampan had a chicken coop lashed to the bulk-head, and most had a floating dog-kennel tied up alongside. (All the dogs are variations of chows— and "chow" sinisterly enough, means "food" in Chinese.)

All the little children had a rope tied round their waist to stop them falling in the water; some of the bigger ones were flying kites from the decks of their houseboats. They all smiled and waved at us. We shouted "Hello" or "Jo Sun" (Chinese for "Good Morning"), and they shouted "Hello" back. One little group of eight-year-olds, paddling past, shouted "Hello Gwei Lo", and burst into torrents of giggles. I waved and called back, but Helen spoke to them crossly. Afterwards she told me that "Hello Gwei Lo" means "Hello Foreign Devil"!

Floating homes in Hong Kong harbour

The children in Kowloon Typhoon Shelter all attended a floating school, but for only half of each day. One shift began at 8 am, and ended at half past twelve: the next started at one thirty, and finished at five o'clock.

All of them, of course, go to school by boat, and at twelve-thirty—change-over time—the traffic jam of sampans at the school landing stage is tremendous. Most of the children wear uniform, the boys, spotless white shirts and blue blazers, the girls, white blouses and gym-slips. They all carried smart black briefcases, which looked very business-like, and strangely incongruous as they leapt from their little sampans on to their school boat.

Brothers and sisters on the morning shift jumped into their places as their mothers turned the boat round and paddled them back home again.

We were being paddled in our taxi-boat to meet the Fung family who live quite close to the school.

Mr and Mrs Fung were leaning over the side waiting to greet us. The children hung back; they were less sure about the lady Gwei Lo (foreign devil) who had come to visit them. Mr Fung Sup Ng—in China the family name comes first—helped me up the ladder, and his wife Mui beckoned me into the little cabin that was their living room. Mr Fung shouted something in Cantonese and all the children, shy and giggling, crept through another small hatch. Mr Fung's father Hin Hong (which means "No Problems"), was in this cabin already and gave Helen and me little wooden stools, about two inches high, to sit on.

I asked them how much accommodation they had for their family of nine; Helen translated the question into Cantonese, and I waited for an answer.

Mr Fung said there was the cabin, their living room, which at night became a bedroom for the five older children. Then he asked Mrs Fung, who was almost as shy as the children, to show me round the rest of the boat. She picked up her baby daughter, whose name was Tai Tei—which means "Bring Brothers"—and put her into a sort of sling on her back, then took me through to the other cabin. This was exactly the same size as the first, but with four bunk beds. Outside, on the stern, open to the air on three sides, was a huge family oven, and right next to that was the lavatory, which consisted of three vertical polished teak boards, shielding the occupant from the gaze of passers-by, and two horizontal polished teak boards, with a hole in the middle.

All this sounds rather squalid, but it wasn't at all. Everything was polished and fresh-looking, and meticulously clean. It didn't even look aggressively neat and orderly, but had that healthy comfortable untidiness that goes with most big families.

Yet there were nine people ranging from Tai Tei, aged three months, to the grandfather, who was about seventy-five, all living, eating and sleeping on a boat which was no more than ten feet wide and thirty feet long—to say nothing of the dog, Kobe.

The boat is not only their home; it is their livelihood as well. Every morning and every evening they cast off from the mooring and go fishing, out beyond the harbour. Some of the wealthier families in the anchorage own big junks with red or brown ribbed sails that look like bats' wings. Some of the boats have diesel engines as well, that once drove London buses!

Junks from Hong Kong's Fragrant Harbour go as far as the Bay of Tonking and then fish in Chinese waters, on condition that they sell a proportion of their catch to Communist China.

Before I left the Fung family's boat, grandfather Hin Hong took me by the hand to show me the most important part of their floating home. In the cabin where the parents slept he opened a trap-door with a polished teak lid.

It was a shrine to Tin Hau, the goddess of the water people.

Goddess of the Water People

Every boat that puts out to sea has a shrine to Tin Hau —the Goddess of the Sea, and Protectress of the Water People. Here the fishermen burn a stick of incense, called a joss-stick, and murmur a prayer before they set sail.

On the coast, there is a huge majestic statue of Tin Hau, looking out to sea from Repulse Bay. Behind her stands the Lifeboat Station, very appropriately, for Tin Hau is traditionally concerned with saving life at sea.

A thousand years ago, the legend tells us, Tin Hau was born, on a day when the ground turned purple, a strange light shone in the sky, and the air was filled with fragrance.

Even as a girl, Tin Hau had strange powers; she could heal the sick, and foretell the future.

Then one day, when her father and brother were out at sea, a violent storm broke out. Tin Hau saw by magic that they were in great danger.

Immediately, by a miracle, she moved over the waters

Shrine to Tin Hau

21

to their rescue, braving the hurricane. She rescued her father from certain death, but for her brother it was too late. He was already drowned.

At once Tin Hau, his sister, dived down to the depths of the ocean, and rescued her brother's body from a watery grave, a fate entirely horrific to all true Chinese.

In her lifetime Tin Hau was honoured as a saint, and after she died prayers were addressed to her, for safety and good weather at sea, while her blessing was sought for every boat putting out of harbour.

And to this day, every year on the twenty-third day of the third moon, the water-people celebrate her birthday.

The Strange World of Oriental Medicine

Thanks to David Carradine, most people in Great Britain know all about Kung Fu, the great Chinese martial art practised so gloriously by Kwai Chang Cain. But how many have heard of Kung Fu's strange and beautiful sister art—the art of Tai Chi?

It is safe to say that anyone practising Tai Chi in a public park in Britain would soon draw a crowd, and might even get arrested as a dangerous lunatic. When our film was being checked by technicians in London, they thought it was all shot in slow motion, until they noticed someone walking past in the background at normal speed.

Every day, Tai Chi practitioners start at first light, in the two main public parks—or indeed, anywhere they can get a little space to move, on this overcrowded island. I once saw an old lady doing her Tai Chi in the space under a fly-over, by a great traffic intersection, quite oblivious of the thousands of cars roaring all round her.

They usually begin by loosely swinging their arms backwards and forwards, then they start to make slow, beautifully-controlled balletic movements, with a rapt look of dedication on their faces.

Tai Chi is not a religion but an exercise, yet like so many Chinese practices, there is an air of mysticism about it.

It is the triumph of mind over matter.

The Chinese say that those who practise Tai Chi will gain the suppleness of a child, the health of a lumber-jack, and the peace of mind of a sage.

But Tai Chi is not the only Chinese solution to the problems of health. What would you say if your doctor advised you to drink the bile of a cobra?

Snakes have been part of Oriental medicine for more than a thousand years. If you eat the flesh of a snake, mixed with that of a civet cat before the start of winter, then you will stay free of coughs and colds and all winter ills.

This, like Tai Chi, is part science, part mysticism, and part superstition.

The snake is a lithe and supple creature, so a medicine made from a snake will, it is claimed, cure your rheumatism, lumbago, arthritis and all the diseases which lock the joints.

The bile of a cobra with orange peel is particularly good for curing dizziness or faintness.

There are shops in Hong Kong that sell nothing but live snakes. From the outside they look rather dull; there's the shop counter in front, with a few bottles with Chinese writing on the labels. The rest of the shop looks something like an old-fashioned ironmongers; the walls are lined from floor to ceiling with business-like heavy drawers.

Open one of these, and you'd be in for a shock. We visited Snake King Yuen's shop in Sai Yan Choi Street on the day a "Consignment" arrived from mainland China.

A boy of about fifteen years old carried in a large box and dumped it unceremoniously in the middle of the floor. He took off the lid, and began systematically to "file" the contents into the wooden drawers.

The *contents* were live, writhing snakes of every sort and size. Handfuls of hooded deadly cobras, strange beautiful black and yellow snakes, the dreaded black mamba, and huge malevolent pythons that had to be folded up to fit them into the drawers.

Once, during the filming, the boy inadvertently dropped a couple of cobras right at the feet of Blue Peter cameraman Ken Westbury—the result was one of the fastest "pans" ever to be photographed!

Snakes are just one facet of the strange mysterious world of Oriental medicine. The chemist's shop, like the snake shop, looks rather dull and business-like. Behind the counter are scores of little drawers and dozens of huge bottles with screw top lids, which contain herbs and strange things like chopped deer's antlers, and dried monkey's liver. People go there with long prescriptions from their doctors, hand-written in beautiful Chinese characters (not like the indecipherable scrawl that you get from most English doctors), although it is not only the doctors who have the power to write prescriptions in Hong Kong.

I went to a chemist with Helen, our interpreter, who

Hong Kong street scene

25

is a young, attractive, and, you would think, Western-ised, kind of girl who has lived in London and travelled all over the world.

"This is something for my mother's headaches," she said, as she produced a long prescription in Chinese.

While the young assistant was chopping up buffalo horn on a huge guillotine, I asked her if she got the prescription from an ordinary doctor like you do in Britain.

"You can do," she said—and then without batting an eyelid, she added: "But this one came from the goddess Tin Hau."

I asked her how the legendary goddess who died a thousand years ago came to be writing a prescription for her mother's headaches.

"Tin Hau didn't write it. My mother went to pray in the Tin Hau Temple, because she kept getting these headaches, and one of the men in the Temple wrote out the prescription for her."

I asked Helen if she really believed this would work.

"I don't know, really— but it's worth trying. You see, my mother has these terrible headaches, and she's tried all the other things," she said, indicating a row of shelves packed with proprietary brands of medicines, just like a chemist at home.

The Chinese, in their way, are very open minded. They have doctors just like us, and they use all the Western medicines.

But lots of people have got better by using the ancient remedies, so they aren't going to turn their backs on a cure that's been going for thousands of years.

Recently we in the West have begun to realise that there may be something in the Oriental medical cures.

Acupuncture, the Chinese method of curing people by sticking needles into their bodies, is beginning to get a following in Europe and America; I know a very respected West Country doctor who recommends acupuncture to his patients!

Yet, somehow, I don't quite see myself taking a prescription from Tin Hau into my chemist's in the Earl's Court Road!

The medicine that has sold more than any other throughout the Orient is an ointment, sold in a little jar with a brightly-coloured wrapper.

It is called Tiger Balm, and it is supposed to cure almost anything. On the instructions, in Chinese, Malay and English, it recommends itself for muscular aches and pains, sprains, rheumatism, insect bites, itching, lumbago, headaches, toothache—etc.

I have no idea how much money the inventor made out of Tiger Balm before he died, but he gave away twenty million U.S. dollars to charity.

He was Aw Boon Haw, the great Chinese philanthropist, who gave away sixty per cent of all his profits. "My money is made from the public, so I should spend for the public!" he declared.

One of the ways he spent money for the public was the creation of the Tiger Balm Gardens in Hong Kong. It is a sort of Oriental Disneyland, with religious statues mixed up with cartoon animals and figures in Chinese history.

It looks really awful to European eyes!

Oriental pop art is ugly and garish at the best of times, but the Tiger Balm Gardens is beyond belief. Horrible brightly-painted gnomes grin up at a huge fat Buddha who leers down at naked ladies sporting

Tiger Balm gardens

about in the strangest positions. They are all made of painted plaster, which is often broken and chipped–and the Chinese love it!

High on the hill overlooking his gnomes and his Buddhas, is a statue to the memory of Aw Boon Haw himself, who died, we are told, in Honolulu at 8.45 pm on 4 September 1954: "Chinese millionaire, philanthropist, and creator of Tiger Balm."

On Saturdays and Sundays the place is packed with thousands of people, all taking photographs of each other, backed by the hideous statues.

Most remarkable of all, perhaps, is the fact that in the centre of it all is Aw Park Mansion, one of the residences of Aw Boon Haw, when he was alive, and still used by Sally Aw, his millionairess daughter.

It must be like living in the middle of Battersea Fun Fair!

Casevac

Even the greatest fan of Tiger Balm would hesitate to try it seriously on a broken arm, and if you lived on one of Hong Kong's other two hundred and thirty-five islands, and were unlucky enough to need skilled medical help in a hurry, you could be in bad trouble. It takes hours to get a seriously injured person from a remote island to a hospital in the heart of Hong Kong island by boat.

The answer to the problem is called Casevac—Casualty Evacuation by Helicopter—and 28 Squadron of the RAF based at Kai Tak operate a round-the-clock Casevac service.

At any hour of the day or night they will turn out

and land on one of the little islands. I'm happy to say I didn't break an arm whilst I was in Hong Kong, but Squadron Leader Puckering and his crew promised me that if I went out to the tiny island of Yim Tin Sai, they would show me just what would happen if I had.

Yim Tin Sai is typical of scores of tiny islands off the shore of mainland China. There is a school, a temple and, more unusually, a Catholic Church, for most of the hundred or so inhabitants are Christian converts. They fish and farm, and live a simple life that has not changed very much in thousands of years. It is odd to think that they are only five minutes by helicopter from the skyscrapers, the neon lights, and the endless roar of Hong Kong traffic.

I stood in the middle of a paddy field, alone except for an old lady wearing the strange curtained hat of the Hakka people. She was muttering words of encouragement—or abuse— to a pair of water buffaloes as she ploughed slowly and laboriously through the deep mud.

Ploughing with water buffaloes

At last I picked up the unmistakable *chucka-chucka-chucka* of threshing rotor blades, and a Whirlwind helicopter suddenly appeared from over the mountains. He soon spotted me, and swung round in a low arc to see if it was going to be possible to land without his wheels disappearing in the mud. The aircraft made one more circle, and then with a down draught that sent the rice straw whirling across the field, came in to land, about ten feet from where I was standing.

Flight Sergeant Tim Bond the Load-master was standing in the doorway talking Squadron Leader John Puckering safely down through the obstacles on the ground.

"All clear port— all clear starboard. Your tail rotor is clear—forward and down. Clear to land. Down five —down four—down three—down two—down one. Leaving the aircraft to pick up casualty."

He leapt out of the helicopter and walked over to where I was crouching from the whirling rotor blade, that seemed about to execute the pair of us. But Flight Sergeant Bond was one of those men who seem so calm and confident that you readily place your life in their hands. He walked over to the door, hoisted me up into the aircraft, and slapped the headset over my ears.

"Everything O.K. Val?" said Squadron Leader Puckering from the cockpit.

"Yes, I think so," I replied.

"Then let's go!"

Flight Sergeant Bond was at the door again.

"All clear port—all clear starboard, sir. Clear to take off."

We surged forward over the paddy field, leaving the old lady with the buffalo a tiny black speck, clutching on to her curtained hat.

We flew over the sea towards the strange undulating mountain ridge called Lion Rock, because it looks just like a lion lying down, its nose pointing towards Hong Kong.

The ridge itself was stark and barren—bare like the surface of the moon. Then suddenly and dramatically we cleared the summit, and Hong Kong, one of the busiest and most sophisticated cities in the world, was spread out before us.

I felt more like a time-traveller than a Casevac!

Ching Ming

"April the fifth is Ching Ming—you won't get much work done on Ching Ming," the man from the Hong Kong Government told us. "It's a public holiday—everything's closed down."

"What on earth's Ching Ming?" we asked.

"It's the day when all the Chinese people go to visit their ancestors' graves," he said.

Edward Barnes the Director tugged his beard. "That doesn't sound very cheerful," he said gloomily.

"On the contrary—it's a very jolly occasion," the government man replied.

So, on 5 April, Helen took the whole Blue Peter unit to the Diamond Hill Urn Cemetery. We had very little idea what we were going to see, and even if we liked it we didn't know if we would be allowed to film. Many Chinese people aren't all that keen on being filmed, and, anyway, even in Britain, a visit to the family grave is a private occasion, where a film crew would not be welcome.

Diamond Hill Urn is a huge cemetery laid out in steep terraces on the side of a hill. All Chinese grave-yards are on the side of a hill, so that the ancestors can look down protectively on their descendants, who climb up to pay them their respects.

Helen was anxious that we should get there in good time, because "all the people go home soon after lunch."

The Director was worried about the crew's lunch. "Don't worry about lunch—I will be able to find you some," Helen said, mysteriously.

"If it only happens once a year in China, we'd look daft if we missed it by eating our lunch," said Ken Westbury.

We needn't have worried. The whole side of the hill was black with people when we arrived. The acrid smell of burning paper was everywhere, and small boys were busy sweeping up bucketfuls of charred embers.

"That's Hell Money," Helen explained. "It's printed pretend-money that is burned as an offering for the dead!"

Flowers were being laid on some of the graves, but not only flowers. Bananas, and cake, and glasses of rice wine were being offered as well.

"The spirit of the food is offered to the ancestors, and the physical food is consumed by the family," Helen went on.

"In other words, you eat it?" I pressed.

"After it has been offered, yes." said Helen.

Several people had pots of red paint which they were using to touch up the lettering on the gravestones. Others were digging out weeds, and generally smarten-ing up the graveside. The smell of joss sticks mingled with that of the burning Hell Money.

But it was not at all a sombre occasion. It was a jolly family outing—in fact a jolly family picnic in a graveyard is the only accurate description of Ching Ming. The food offerings were placed on the grave, and after a decent interval the whole family tucked in. And it wasn't restricted to the odd cake and banana either. We saw a whole roast sucking pig carried up the steep stairs.

We asked everybody's permission before we filmed, and very few refused. One family had an enormous picnic, with a table cloth, a primus stove, and a steam boat bubbling away. A steam boat is a cauldron of boiling water that you can cook things in at the table, and then you fish out the food with chopsticks.

Helen asked in Chinese if it was O.K. to film. Then she turned to us, and said: "He says yes, and afterwards would the whole crew like to join them for Ching Ming?"

We all sat round cross-legged in the sun. Our host gave us chopsticks, and told us to help ourselves. If any of us seemed reluctant he produced huge chunks of pork from the steam-boat, and laid them on our plates.

It was quite the happiest visit to a grave I'd ever seen.

Helen fished a huge Pacific prawn out of the boiling cauldron, and turned to Ken Westbury and said: "I told you we'd be all right for lunch!"

China Tea

Hong Kong harbour throbbed with activity, much as it does today, when the colony developed as a trading base, but just over a hundred years ago the most important shipping in the magnificent harbour were the tall clippers that carried the tea to London.

Tea was the magnet that drew English merchants to China.

I found that in Hong Kong, people leading a British way of life lived alongside millions of Chinese, following age-old traditions, but the British and the Chinese, in Hong Kong and the world over, are great tea drinkers.

Tea in China is served in a different way, poured into little porcelain "china" cups, without milk and sugar. I drank it like that, which seems strange at first, but the clear golden brew is refreshing and delicious.

Chinese tea cup

The Chinese claim to have invented tea, nearly five thousand years ago.

The Emperor Shen Nung, they say, was a great hygiene addict, and always insisted on boiling his drinking water. One day, as the pot bubbled, a few leaves from the branches on the fire fell into the water.

They were tea leaves—and the flavour of the liquid was so delicate and agreeable, the Emperor drank tea from then onwards.

So did all his subjects. Before long, all the Chinese, from Emperor to peasant, loved nothing better than gathering round a tea-table, sipping the honey-coloured liquid, in a calm, meditative, civilised manner.

So for nearly five thousand years, the Chinese have grown tea—no longer relying on a few chance leaves blowing from the fire. They have dried it, blended it, tasted it and marketed it.

Inside a teashop

I went into a dark, interesting shop, lined with chests full of all varieties of tea, the contents described in black Chinese characters. In Hong Kong, tea is sold by experts to experts, and drunk all round the clock, so that the streets smell of jasmin tea, all day and all night.

Westerners in China discovered the magic of tea, and took it home to Europe. Three hundred years ago, it reached England.

Catherine of Braganza, the Portuguese wife of King Charles II introduced tea into court circles in England. It was tried as a curiosity, or as a medicine. "Prepared and drunk with milk and water, it strengtheneth the inward parts", a doctor claimed.

In England, from the start, tea was taken with milk.

A century later, the tea-table was a favourite luxury in every wealthy home. Furnished with gleaming silver and transparent china tea-cups, it was the centre of the family gathering every evening.

After yet another century, tea drinking had spread to everybody. Tea—the warm, comforting, non-alcoholic beverage—had become the great stand-by of the British people.

The drink became more and more popular; and British merchants in the colony of Hong Kong were eager to meet the demand.

The tall tea clipper was designed especially, with slim lines, high masts, and an enormous spread of sail, to catch every breeze, for speed was all-important. The fresher the tea, the better, and the higher the price on the London market. Too long at sea spoiled the flavour.

The precious tea was brought to Hong Kong from mainland China, and loaded into the clippers. Every year seven or eight ships left the harbour on the same tide, loaded with that season's crop of tea, and bound for Britain.

Then no more would be heard of them, as they tossed and strained on their six-thousand-mile voyage.

In London, the tea merchants waited in desperate impatience for news. The man whose cargo was unloaded first could sell it at an extra ten shillings a pound above the rest, and merchants bet enormous sums on the result of the race.

The master and crew of the clipper piled on sail, and raced ahead—*they* would get a bonus of £500 to share, if they were the first ship home.

At last the leader reached the English Channel, sometimes only minutes ahead of her nearest rival, and others not far behind. In 1866 the *Taeping* was only ten minutes ahead of the *Ariel*, but the race was not over yet.

In London the nightwatchman at the warehouse waited, watching the wind clock, connected to a weather vane on the roof. When it read south-west, the wind to bring the ships home, a messenger leapt on a horse and galloped to tell the merchants sleeping at home.

And one merchant arrived, breathless and triumphant, to welcome his ship—the winner!

The tea chests were trundled ashore, and Britain could breathe a sigh of relief. The tea supply for the next year had begun to arrive.

The tea clipper was the last splendid beautiful achievement of the age of sail. The journey from Canton, or Hong Kong, could be made in an incredible ninety-seven days. But the race did not last long. The age of the sailing clipper was over as soon as steamships could make the voyage in a fraction of the time. The tea-drinking British established tea plantations in India and Ceylon, so that China was no longer the only source of supply.

But China tea has always been demanded by the connoisseur, and drunk without milk or sugar to disturb its delicate fragrance.

The Land of Perpetual Harvest

Across the harbour from Hong Kong, and behind its twin city of Kowloon, is a wide stretch of open countryside.

Here Chinese men and women, in black cotton suits work in the rice fields, or guide the placid buffaloes calmly through the meadows. It is another world from noisy, throbbing, bustling Hong Kong.

This is the New Territories, land leased from China by Britain in 1898 for ninety-nine years, and here time has stood still, and the old way of life continued, in a way that has not been possible in revolution-torn mainland China.

The green and pleasant countryside is so fertile the region was once known as "The Emperor's Rice Bowl". Today it could be called Hong Kong's market garden; but although nearly half the food for Hong Kong's four million inhabitants is grown there, the scene looked like a landscape painting of rural China, centuries ago.

The men in the fields, and the women working alongside them, wearing straw hats, with black fringes hanging over the wide brims, are called the Hakka people—the Strangers— but they have been there for five hundred years.

The names of the scattered villages reflect their quiet prosperity, though walls have been built round them, as a protection against marauders from the hills.

I went to visit the walled village of Kam Tin— Perpetual Harvest. Centuries before the Hakka people arrived, the Tang family lived there, and I was told a story about them.

Long ago the Emperor Sung Ko Chung took as his second wife the gentle and beautiful Fu Cheng, who was a talented painter. They had a daughter called Tsung Kei. War broke into their quiet lives; soldiers attacked the palace, and the royal family were forced to flee, with the ten-year-old Princess Tsung Kei.

In the confusion the little girl got lost. Lonely and frightened, she looked over the countryside for help. In the distance she saw a military camp flying the Emperor's flag, so she made her way towards it.

The Emperor was not there—only his general, Tang

Working in the rice fields

Yuen Luen. He received Tsung Kei kindly, though she did not tell him who she was. He took her back to his home at Kam Tin, and there she was brought up with his family, his eldest son Tang Tze Ming, and his other children.

When they grew up, Tang Tze Ming and Princess Tsung Kei were married. They were happy and the marriage was blessed with four sons.

Many years passed; peace was restored to the troubled land, and a new Emperor, grandson of Sung Ko Chung, now ruled. Tsung Kei, who had become a widow, went to court with her four sons, and made herself known to the Emperor.

He greeted them with honour and kindness. He gave the sons posts at court, and grants of land near Kam Tin; he bestowed on Tsung Kei the honourable title of Emperor's Aunt, and made her a gift of pictures painted by her mother, the artist Fu Cheng, that had been treasured at the palace.

At long last Tsung Kei, now eighty-seven years old, lay at the point of death. She was told she would be ceremoniously buried in a nearby lion-shaped hill. "But tell us," she was asked, "will you be buried by the lion's head, which will mean that your descendants will be great men, or by his tail, which will mean they are humble people?"

The Princess raised herself up on her pillows. "I do not want my descendants to become great," she declared. "I was an Emperor's daughter, and yet I was in danger of my life. I want my children's children to enjoy peaceful lives, with enough rice and fish to eat for ever. If they have that they should be content."

That was nearly nine hundred years ago. The

Emperor's Aunt was buried far away from Kam Tin, but on a hillside close at hand there is a monument to her, where her memory is honoured by her descendants, who, to this day, live in the village nearby.

And everyone who lives there today is a descendant of the Princess: they are all members of one family, and they are all called Tang.

We were very fortunate, because Helen who took me to Kam Tin and told me its stories is herself a member of the Tang family. She led me through the beautiful wrought iron gates, strong enough to resist any invader, which guard the only entrance through the solid stone walls.

The main street is about four feet wide, and stretches from the gate right into the centre of the village to the Temple at the far end. I walked the whole length of it with Helen, who was greeted by everybody as they passed by: everyone, of course, was some sort of relation.

"That's my old Great Auntie," she said, as we passed an aged crone with a walnut face and black curtained hat. She was smoking a silver pipe, and looked as though she had stepped out of Ancient China.

Helen, on the other hand, looked as if she had stepped straight out of Vogue. Her smart black trousers, red and white patterned shirt and black shiny belt, seemed to put her in a different world from all the rest of her people, but it didn't seem to worry Helen, nor anyone else, as far as I could see.

Her elder brother appeared, wearing a smart European suit, and said formally: "You are very welcome here."

Another girl wearing modern European clothes said something to Helen in Chinese, and they both giggled.

Temple altar in Kam Tin

"That's my young sister. She was Miss Hong Kong last year."

A grey-haired lady, wearing the traditional black trouser suit of the Chinese, came round the corner, carrying a little girl about three years old. They both had really beautiful faces; the older woman grey-haired, lined and brown, with strong noble bones, and the little girl with jet black hair and devastating dark brown eyes, much rounder than the average Chinese.

They all greeted each other with hugs and kisses and volumes of Chinese.

"This is my mother—and this is my daughter, Louise. Her father is an Englishman," said Helen.

We all walked on up the narrow street together, and without ceasing their conversation, walked into the little Temple. Helen's mother with little Louise still in her arms lit a joss stick and stuck it in the sand before the altar.

"It is in honour of my ancestor," Helen explained. "I am not allowed to do it any more, because I have gone away from the village."

The Death of a Queen

While I was in Hong Kong, I was very anxious to see something that had nothing to do with the people of Hong Kong, though it was in Hong Kong harbour.

I wanted to go out to see the huge dark twisted mass of metal, half submerged under the sea, that is all that remains of the original *Queen Elizabeth*, in her day the biggest and most luxurious ocean liner in the world.

It was a personal affair for me, because I sailed on her myself, in her great days. Years ago I made a voyage for Blue Peter, from Southampton to Cherbourg.

It was, I remember, a beautiful spring day, and nothing seemed more proud and gleaming and confident than the *Queen Elizabeth* as she sailed down the Solent that May morning. I stood with the Captain and the Pilot on the bridge as they nonchalantly steered the gigantic liner out of port. I played deck quoits with Christopher Trace, who was on Blue Peter in those days, and ate the most enormous meals in the glittering restaurant. There were endless parties, and dances. No one swam in the big open air swimming pool, because it was early May—but it was there if anyone fancied it.

We both had huge staterooms, and could, if we needed, have called on the services of doctors, dentists, hairdressers, beauticians, chiropodists and manicurists. Meals and drinks would arrive at our rooms at the push of a bell.

Soon after that trip people decided that they would rather fly to New York in average discomfort taking five hours, than sail in the lap of luxury (Atlantic swell permitting) in five days.

The great Queen began a life of exile and humiliation. She was sold to American speculators, who first tried to turn her into a tourist attraction, and then into a centre for exhibitions and conventions. Both ventures failed miserably.

In September 1970 she was brought to Hong Kong harbour by a Chinese shipping magnate, who had plans to make her into a floating University, renaming her "Seawise University".

It was then that it seemed as if the old Queen had had enough!

On 9 January 1972 a mysterious fire broke out in her hold. Soon the whole ship was alight, and despite all the efforts of the Hong Kong Fire Brigade, it became obvious that the liner was doomed. For five days and nights she blazed, sending up a huge column of black smoke. Soon it was all over, and the *Queen Elizabeth* lay at the bottom of Hong Kong harbour.

Strangely enough, it was on Blue Peter that the first live pictures of the dying ship were shown in Britain.

And so, nine years after that May morning, I was filming what remained of her, by another strange co-incidence with the same director and the same camera-man . . . I looked at her and thought: that twisted piece of chrome could have been the ladder into the swimming pool: that half-submerged deck might have been where Christopher Trace cheated at deck quoits—or was it I that cheated?

And now she was being broken up for scrap. It takes a long time to cut up and carry away thousands of tons of ocean liner, but every day she was getting a little smaller, and soon even the rusting hulk was doomed to disappear.

It was rumoured that the salvage was being sold across the border into mainland China; it seemed odd to think that the imperial grandeur of the RMS *Queen Elizabeth* was going to end her days as scrap in Communist China.

The China Border

Even apart from the *Queen Elizabeth*, there is so much trade and contact between Hong Kong and Communist China, I was amazed.

In the Central District, the commercial heart of Hong Kong, the Bank of China looks like all the other skyscraper blocks, in spite of the stone Chinese lions guarding the doorway. In half a dozen places, department stores are filled with goods sent from China.

The border with mainland China is only twenty-five miles from Hong Kong, along the course of a meandering river.

At Lok Ma Chau there is an observation post which is crowded with tourists from all nations—Japanese, Americans, Europeans—who flock there to point out *real* Chinese fields, and *real* Chinese Communist peasants working in them.

The strange thing is, the country the other side of the border looks exactly the same as it does on the Hong Kong side.

At Sha Tau Kok, the international boundary actually runs across the main street, and the villagers cross it freely in both directions.

The day of our expedition to the Border, it rained harder and longer than I can ever remember. We started off very early in the morning and drove through the pitch darkness; it was raining so hard that the windscreen wipers at double speed couldn't cope with it, so we crawled with headlights full on, through the Harbour Tunnel to the New Territories, and through the Lion Rock Tunnel into the country.

We stopped at various police posts on the way, where dripping oilskin-clad guards inspected our passes. Eventually we drove up the hill to the final police post at Man Kam To. Dawn was just breaking as we got the equipment out of the car, and carried it up to the flat roof.

A very wet Gurkha soldier was standing looking out towards China, his automatic rifle slung upside down, to protect it from the rain.

Below us flowed the Sham Chun River, which marks the beginning of Communist China. On either side were rice paddies, and only the pillboxes every five hundred yards on the Chinese side betrayed the fact that it was a border. Things are calmer on the Border these days, but not so long ago Chinese refugees were shot down from those pillboxes, as they tried to escape across the rice fields to the freedom of Hong Kong.

Running across the river was a temporary Bailey Bridge, about ten feet wide. On the Chinese side another wet sentry was standing with inverted rifle, looking towards our post.

Then, as the light came up, we saw a line of Chinese workers in traditional baggy pants and large coolie hats walking in single file across the bridge. Neither sentry paid any attention. It looked, as the rain drove down diagonally, like an ancient Chinese picture.

"They come every day," explained our sentry. "The Border runs straight through the farm, so both sides have agreed to let them carry on farming."

A few minutes later a Chinese voice from the Hong Kong side shouted something over a loudspeaker. There was a pause, then a loudspeaker voice replied from the China side.

"What's going on?" I asked, suddenly alarmed.

"Wait," said the sentry.

Then a herd of strange white creatures began to trickle across the bridge. I peered through the driving rain.

"Pigs?" I asked—but I didn't really believe it.

I bought this zoom lens for my camera and tried it out in Hong Kong Harbour

A lesson on the floating school at the Kowloon typhoon shelter

The Festival of Ching Ming when the Chinese visit the graves of their ancestors

This working mother has no baby sitting problems!

Kobe, the Fung family dog, in his kennel outside the home

Helen and I visit the Fung family on board their floating home

A paint-in with children of the New Method School

Another of my purchases, an oiled paper umbrella –
three dollars if it's dry – six if it's raining!

One of Helen's older relatives in the walled village of Kam Tin

The Blue Peter film crew join in the Festival of
St Nicholas at Siggiewi

Seeing Valletta in a Karrozzin

The Maltese stored their grain beneath these stones –
in case of siege!

I try to speak with the voice of the oracle in the underground temple of the Hypogeum

Preparing for the Festival with the Farrugia family

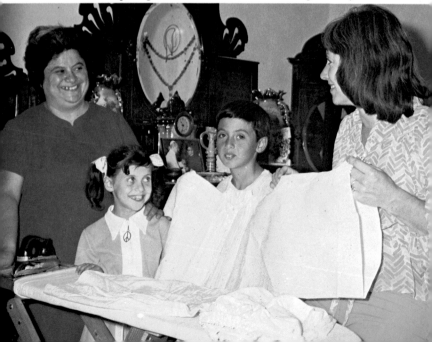

The sentry told me that hundreds of pigs were driven across every morning, destined to be eaten that night in Hong Kong.

The farm workers in the New Territories produce only half the vegetables, pigs and cattle needed to feed Hong Kong—the rest has to be imported, and most of it comes from Communist China.

Once there was a daily air service from Hong Kong to Canton, the biggest town in South China, but that stopped twenty-five years ago. Rails from the station at Kowloon opposite the harbour run straight to Canton. Then—theoretically—passengers can cross China by train, link up with the Trans-Siberian Railway over Russia, and so into Europe.

In fact, today, twenty-two miles from the starting point, every passenger must leave the train, at the border station of Lo Wu.

On that same drenching morning I went to meet Anthony Lawrence at Lo Wu. Until recently Tony was the BBC's Far East correspondent, and he probably knows more about China and Hong Kong than any other European.

We were standing under our umbrellas in the middle of the narrow track as the train from Hong Kong arrived. The people piled off, carrying suitcases and plastic bags. They all filed into a door marked "To Mainland China", where they went through Hong Kong Customs and Immigration. Then they came out of another door and walked along the railway track over the bridge which crossed the river, until they came to another train, which was waiting to take them to China.

Tony told me that there are three trains a day from

China which connect with Hong Kong. I asked him what kind of people cross the border.

"Many of them are just ordinary simple people visiting their relatives. Providing they have an exit permit and a re-entry permit they can cross from one side to the other. You see, they are all Cantonese—the same people on both sides of the border."

"You see that old chap there," he said, pointing to a man with long white moustaches, carrying a shoulder-pole hung with pots and pans half-covered in black plastic to protect it from the drenching rain. "He's probably visiting a brother or a sister, and he's taking some of the goods from capitalist Hong Kong which aren't so easy to come by in Communist China."

"What is it like on the mainland?" I asked him.

"Well, of course, the countryside is exactly the same; it is in the towns you find the difference—so very much more regular and monotonous and well scrubbed, after the wild, colourful, capitalistic Disneyland of Hong Kong. Life is much more disciplined, but everyone is clad, they have enough to eat, and they have shelter and that seems to suit quite a lot of people there."

"But not everyone," I said. "Or they wouldn't risk death swimming through shark-infested waters to get away."

"No. The impatient young men who see themselves working as peasants for life sometimes find that hard to accept, and a lot of them try to get away."

"Some people do emigrate legally, don't they?" I asked.

"If you're old and disabled, oh, yes. They'll let you get out very easily then. But if you're a young

Old man with shoulder-pole

51

able-bodied chap whose work is needed on the country-side, they won't let you go. The only way is to risk being shot crossing the border, or brave the sharks and the long swim across Deep Bay."

I asked Tony what he thought would happen when, in twenty-three years' time, Britain's lease on the New Territories fell through. Would half Hong Kong go back to China?

"That's very hard to say. The Chinese don't acknowledge the lease anyway, and if they wanted to, they could take back Hong Kong any time they liked. But so far it has suited them to have Hong Kong as a back door to the West, and when the lease is up, they may say, 'Well, it's working very well: we get a lot of foreign currency through the trade across the Border—so let the place tick over.' That's what a lot of people hope—but with China, no one can ever be sure."

So the strange story of Hong Kong might all be over in twenty-three years' time, with everything swallowed up into the vast acres of Mainland China.

If it goes, it will be the end of the final chapter of the British Empire East of Suez.

But of Hong Kong's four million citizens, 98% are Chinese and over half are under twenty-one. Perhaps that is why this island is not so concerned with the past, nor anxious about the distant future. I found the people of Hong Kong committed to confident planning for tomorrow, while enjoying every second of their bustling, thrusting varied life of today.

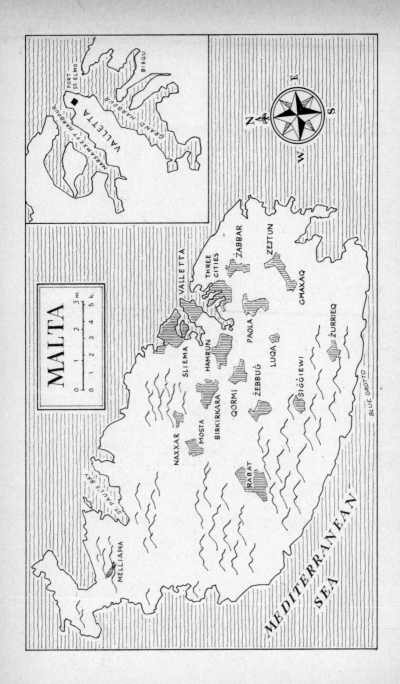

MALTA

The Honey Island

The name Malta, I was told, comes from Mellita, a word which means honey, and it is very appropriate.

Not only is Maltese honey, made from orange blossom and wild thyme in the warm days of early summer, absolutely delicious—but the whole island seems a beautiful honey colour.

In the countryside the hot dry landscape, without lakes or rivers, and with sparse vegetation, is baked golden brown, like a cake that is perfectly cooked. In the towns pale golden walls present a solid blank façade to the passer-by. Only a massive door, adorned with a magnificent brass dolphin door knocker, shows the way into the homes of some of the most hospitable people in the world.

I meet the Farrugia Family

On the south-western part of the island stands one of Malta's many honey-coloured villages, called Siggiewi.

It is much like any other small country village in Malta, with its fair share of churches, statues and houses—all of them, of course, built from the local honey-hued limestone.

The Maltese people are very religious—and they take any opportunity to have a party. These two aspects of Malta come together at festival time. Each village has its own festival once a year, on the special feast day to which their own church is dedicated. Everyone joins in, and people come in from neighbouring villages, to make sure it isn't as good as their festival was. So the feast day is a great occasion, and preparations are begun in good time.

The church at Siggiewi is dedicated to St Nicholas whose festival falls on 23 June, so when I got to the village a week before, I found everybody was already terribly busy.

"Gentlemen, can we go from the horn entry again— only this time with much more attack. Are you ready? One – two – ."

I had arrived in Siggiewi on band practice night; there were only seven days to go in the count-down for the festival, so concentration was pretty fierce.

The band is a great feature of all Maltese festivals; it leads all the processions, as well as playing a concert in the village square, and like everyone else associated with the festival the musicians were all working-men, who had to practise in their spare time.

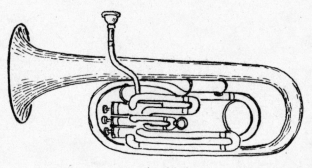

An althorn

I had come specially to meet the althorn player, Mr Nick Farrugia, not only to hear him play the althorn, which he did very well, but because he had promised to take me home to meet his family who were also preparing for the festival.

Mrs Farrugia, a lovely dark-eyed lady with a broad bosom and an even broader smile was one of the most welcoming people I've ever met in my life. Jane Tarleton, the Blue Peter Research Assistant, said: "She makes you feel at home before you've got half a leg round the door," and that just about sums her up. When I arrived she was busy ironing a cotta for Beppe, who was an altar boy at the church, and would be walking beside the statue of St Nicholas in the great procession, carrying a candle. The cotta had hundreds of pleats, and six inches of Maltese lace at the bottom, so the ironing needed a lot of concentration.

Eleven-year-old Beppe was looking on with a slightly anxious expression, as his mother kept darting between the ironing board and Rita, Beppe's eight-year-old sister, who was in the middle of a fitting for the dress that she was going to wear on the day. Rita had big dark eyes and a wicked smile. She refused to speak English at first, although she understood everything that was going on. At the moment she was showing a cheerfully resigned spirit, as her mother dashed between her and the ironing board.

The whole family (including Rita) spoke excellent English. This is a compulsory subject at school, partly because the Maltese language is not spoken anywhere else in the world. The two elder girls, Mary aged eighteen, and Joyce aged nineteen were not actually taking part in the procession, but like everyone else in the village, they were part of the Siggiewi Festival. Proudly and demurely they showed me the dresses that they each would wear for the three high days of the festival.

The eldest boy, sixteen-year-old Nicholas (very

Beppe dressed for the procession

59

good-looking and delightfully unaware of it!) popped his head round the door to be introduced. He bowed politely, but soon disappeared before the welter of feminine activity!

Although Mrs Farrugia and her daughters pressed us to stay, we thought it would be kinder to let them get on with their preparations, but we promised to come back again before the big day.

Malta, G.C.

On the big day, the village is decked out with flags and decorations. Prominent among them is Malta's own red and white flag, proudly displaying on its white background the emblem of the Order of the George Cross, Britain's highest award for civilian bravery.

Flag of Malta

The name of the island in full is Malta, G.C., because just over thirty years ago Malta was given a medal—the only time that this has ever happened to an island.

It happened during the Second World War, when Britain alone was standing up to the threat of Nazi conquest of Europe.

Malta was at the very heart of it all—France, Italy, North Africa and Greece were all under enemy control. Malta was a vital base for the British, so the enemy was determined to overcome the island.

Bomber planes threatened the airfields, the harbour, and every man, woman and child on Malta. Enemy ships pressed home the attack, and a rigid blockade cut off all supplies of food, fuel and ammunition.

Occupation and invasion were an hourly peril.

Malta was badly equipped, with not nearly enough planes to defend her, but three fighter aircraft were discovered, packed in cases in an obscure naval store-room. Somehow they were reassembled, trundled out and used to resist every attack. The Maltese people called them *Faith*, *Hope* and *Charity*.

1942 was the desperate year. In March and April twice as many bombs fell on Malta as on London in the whole of the worst year of the war.

Some people may have remembered the words of a man who six hundred years before, had described Malta as "A rock in the midst of the sea, far from help and comfort!"

The Maltese people hung on grimly, waiting for relief to come.

Such was their bravery, that on 15 April 1942 they received a message from King George VI :

Faith, Hope *and* Charity, *the famous fighter aircraft of World War II*

"To honour her brave people, I award the George Cross to the Island Fortress of Malta, to bear witness to a heroism and devotion that will long be famous in history."

The King had decided that the George Cross should be awarded, not just to one person but to the whole island and everybody on it.

The position of the George Cross Island soon became desperate. Malta was threatened with starvation or surrender—help *must* get through!

In August the British High Command planned a convoy, under the code name *Pedestal*—fourteen merchant ships were loaded with four months' supplies —food—flour—drink—ammunition. The tanker *Ohio*, American built with a British crew, carried the vital oil.

The convoy was guarded by three aircraft carriers, two battleships, six cruisers and twenty-four destroyers. For air cover, overhead circled one hundred and thirty-six fighters, thirty-eight bombers, and sixteen reconnaissance aircraft.

The Relief of Malta was Top Priority!

On 10 August, the convoy steamed through the Straits of Gibraltar. Spanish fishing boats sighted it, and informed the enemy. They were ready—two hundred and eighty bombers, torpedo boats, U-boats and destroyers swarmed around, attacking and harassing the convoy for every mile of its thousand-mile journey eastward through the Mediterranean.

The convoy was thinned out appallingly—ship after ship was sunk. The *Ohio* was damaged, and set on fire, but she managed to limp on. Fifty miles from Malta dive bombers attacked in force, but were beaten off.

Then tugs went out, and took her in tow.

On 15 August, the *Ohio* was tugged into Valletta Harbour in Malta, still carrying her all-important cargo of oil, while the people of Malta gathered on the ramparts and cheered her rapturously.

Of the convoy *Pedestal*, one carrier, two cruisers, one destroyer, countless aircraft and nine of the original fourteen supply ships had been lost.

The tide of war turned—three years later the British were victorious.

Today Malta is not owned by Britain any more; but she still bears the marks of that great siege, and although the island is independent, she still proudly carries the special title, Malta, G.C.

The Great Siege

There is a plaque commemorating the award of the George Cross in the main street of Malta's capital, Valletta. The city was named after the island's greatest hero, La Valette, who won fame and glory in another siege, almost four hundred years before the Second World War.

Jean Parisot de la Valette was a Frenchman, from a wealthy noble family, who joined the Order of the Knights of St John of Jerusalem when he was twenty years old. From then on, he never went back home, or back to France; the Order was his career and his whole life.

The Order had been founded five hundred years earlier, to give aid and comfort to Christian pilgrims to the Holy Land. The Saracens—the Mohammedan Turks—attacked the pilgrims, who needed armed guards to protect them. The Order became a company of warrior monks, wearing armour, pledged to spend their whole lives at war with the infidel.

Soon the Turks, representing Islam, and the Knights of St John, representing Christendom, were at perpetual war throughout the Mediterranean, on land and sea.

La Valette became a great seaman, who commanded the Order's battle fleet. "He is a very handsome man, tall and calm and unemotional, speaking several languages fluently—Italian, Spanish, Greek, Arabic and Turkish," someone wrote.

His great companion in the Order was an Englishman, Sir Oliver Starkey.

In one battle, the Turks captured the Knights' ship, and La Valette, with all his crew, were made galley slaves. He was forty-seven years old, and for a year, chained to his oar, he lived a life of almost intolerable hardship.

The Turkish Commander was the Admiral Dragut, renowned as the great enemy of the Knights, and known as the Sword of Islam.

La Valette was ransomed, and resumed his rank. Then, after more fighting, it happened that Dragut was made captive in his turn.

"Monsieur Dragut, it is the fortune of war," said La Valette.

"And a change of fortune," replied Dragut grimly. But he too survived slavery, and went back to high command, and unending war.

La Valette went to Malta with the Knights because the Turks had driven them from their other bases, and the barren island was the only home they could find.

"I am at Malta—of all places in the world!" wrote

Sir Oliver Starkey, ruefully.

When La Valette was sixty-three years old, he became Grand Master of the Order of the Knights of St John, and ruler of Malta. He was certain the Turks would attack Malta in force, to drive the Knights from their last haven, and then use the island as a base to attack Europe. He made his headquarters at Birgu, overlooking the harbour.

"We must watch and wait, because we do not know the day they will come," La Valette warned his Knights.

For years they waited. Then one spring day in 1565, the look-out shouted. A black speck on the horizon— it grew and grew! A faraway rhythm, getting louder! It was the drums of two hundred Turkish galleys, setting the time for the rowers—forty thousand Turkish troops were speeding against Malta. Soon the enemy forces were gathered, ready to do battle.

Turkish galley

The Grand Harbour at Malta is divided into two by a narrow peninsula, which in those days was just a barren rock, with a small fortress, called St Elmo, at the tip. Before the Turks could attack La Valette's headquarters across the harbour at Birgu, they had to take St Elmo.

"It will take less than a week!" declared the Turkish commanders. But across the water, the seventy-year-old La Valette warned his men: "St Elmo is the key to Malta."

He had five hundred and forty knights and nine thousand men-at-arms under his command—less than a quarter of the Turkish force. He sent frantic calls for help to every Christian monarch in Europe, and prepared to hold on doggedly until it arrived.

As the Turks lined up their men and guns, ready to attack, still more ships were seen. The Turks cheered, and shouted: "Dragut—Dragut has arrived!" Their great Admiral, the Sword of Islam, now eighty years old, had come to take command.

Yet valiant though he was, he was fatalistic about the future. "I have felt in this island the shadow of the wing of death," he murmured. "It is written that one of these days I too shall die in the territory of the Knights."

Now the walls of St Elmo were bombarded by Turkish cannon all day long, day after day. Relentlessly the siege continued, and the garrison was hard pressed. Whenever a breach was made in the walls, the defenders rushed to thrust back the wave of Turkish troops, who all fiercely yelled one word: "Allah!"

I stood on the narrow stone bridge, leading to the main gate of the fortress, over a wide, deep moat, and thought of the terrible conflict that had raged in this very place.

The Turks tried to put assault ladders against the walls, and shot with muskets. When it came to hand-to-hand fighting, their chief weapon was the terrible scimitar, with its deadly crescent blade, which had long been the most dreaded weapon in their armoury. Both Knights and Turks used halberds, combined spears and battle-axes, with horrible and sinister war-heads. Siege warfare was a frightful and blood-thirsty business.

The Turks wore turbans, and loose flowing robes: these inspired La Valette to invent the Knights' most ingenious weapon, a firework hoop. Wooden rings were packed with gunpowder and rags soaked in oil and pitch. They were set alight and hurled blazing over the walls at the attackers. The Turks tripped and fell, their long robes caught fire and panic spread.

Not only were the weapons frightful, but the Knights fought in armour, often weighing as much as a hundred pounds. They must have felt roasted alive, or dead with exhaustion, after fighting for eight hours on end, under the burning summer sun.

It was not a pretty war—too much was at stake. Each side felt committed to a holy war they were bound to win. There was a great deal of courage and endurance, but there was bloodshed and misery and horror, just like any war.

The garrison defending St Elmo knew it would fall in the end; they were only fighting for time. They hoped to delay the Turks from advancing on to La Valette's headquarters long enough for him to organise his own defences. Then the Knights in St Elmo wrote

A Knight of St John

69

A Turkish soldier

70

to La Valette. "Give us orders to withdraw," they asked, "then we can carry on fighting. Do not let us waste our lives here to no purpose!"

La Valette knew the enormous value of every day gained. He wrote back: "I will send a relief force this evening, and you may leave in their boats. I shall feel more confident when I know that the fort, upon which the safety of the island depends, is held by men whom I can trust implicitly."

The Knights were furious, their honour outraged. If anyone was to stay and fight it out—they would! St Elmo was *their* fortress, and they would stay till the very end.

The garrison thought the end was very near, but in fact they hung on for another sixteen incredible days, although they were now sealed off from all help. The attacks became more and more devastating, the breaches in the walls grew wider, and the moat filled with piles of bodies.

Eventually the garrison knew they could hold out for just one more day—only a handful of men were left alive. They made their way to the chapel, in the heart of the fortress, and prayed. They burned all the sacred objects from the chapel, so that the heathen Turks would have no booty to mock and triumph over. They rang the chapel bell, to say farewell to La Valette and their brothers over the harbour, who would be attacked next.

And they waited until morning, when the last attack came. The few remaining Knights and men-at-arms were killed in front of the chapel. A Turkish soldier hauled down the flag of St John. Dragut had been mortally wounded in the fighting, but he lingered long enough to be told that St Elmo had fallen. Soon the crescent flag of Islam flew over the ruins of the fort.

What followed was the most horrifying incident of the war. The Turks thought they would frighten the defenders of Birgu into giving up by an impressive display of cruelty. They cut off the heads of the slaughtered Knights and put their bodies into the sea, on rafts. They knew the headless bodies would drift across the harbour on the current, to reach La Valette.

When the rafts reached him, he did not hesitate. Calmly and ruthlessly he ordered that all the Turkish prisoners should be killed and beheaded. Then the guns of Birgu opened fire on the Turkish camp, firing the heads of the Turkish prisoners instead of cannon balls. It was a sign, if one were needed, that from now on, no mercy would be given, since none could be expected!

The fortress of St Elmo

Although the Knights had lost St Elmo, the victory had cost the Turks the lives of eight thousand of their men—and Dragut. They had expected St Elmo would fall in a week—it had held out for thirty-one days, and that had given La Valette time—time to strengthen his garrison, and gather together his arms. Time to bring in forty thousand casks of water, and food for several weeks. Time to send out more urgent appeals to Europe for help. La Valette was ready for battle, and there would be no surrender.

Every night after the day's hard fighting, the Turks withdrew to their comfortable camp across the harbour, but they were dismayed and wretched, for they had believed they would be masters of Malta in a few weeks, yet after four months the Knights were somehow holding on, day after day.

Wherever fighting was fiercest, La Valette was in the thick of it. In one attack, his own nephew, one of the Knights, was killed in action, and the rest offered him sympathy, but he declared staunchly: "All the Knights are my children, and they are all equally dear to me. And soon we must all die, beneath these ruins." For now it was the end of August, and the Knights despaired of any relief arriving.

Then, one day, there was no assault at daybreak. There was no fighting. The Knights looked out from their battered desolate stronghold. The Turks were striking camp, and their ships were moving away.

The relief from Sicily had arrived in the north of the island, and struck the Turks in the rear. After one last hideous and bloody battle, the Turks had given way—and they were sailing back to Turkey.

The Turks had gone, and Malta was safe. Across the

harbour, the Cross of St John flew again over the pile of stones that had once been the fortress of St Elmo. As the victory bells pealed out, La Valette gave Birgu a new name—Vittoriosa, the victorious city.

"In spite of our losses," La Valette declared, "let us rejoice on this day—September the eighth—the Feast of Our Lady of Victories!"

La Valette, Grand Master of the Order

The Grand Master, La Valette, was an old man now, a legend in his lifetime, but he had one task left. He was determined to make Malta an impregnable fortress, safe from every attack in the future.

All the walls and defences in the old forts and cities were rebuilt; an aqueduct, which survives to this day, was made to carry water across the island, and granaries were constructed, so that Malta would have safe supplies of water and grain if ever again she was besieged.

On the neck of land that ended in St Elmo, walls began to rise, and streets appeared. La Valette had a little hut made, and lived there to supervise all the work in the new city.

It was to be called Valletta.

But his old enemy was not forgotten, for the point across the harbour, where he had landed, was now always called Dragut point.

At last La Valette fell ill, and died. Black-draped galleys carried his body across the harbour, and he was laid to rest in Valletta, the new city that was his namesake.

His body lies now in the crypt of the cathedral of St John. His friend Oliver Starkey lies near him, and on his tomb is carved an epitaph that Oliver Starkey composed for him: "Here lies La Valette, worthy of eternal honour. He who was once the scourge of Africa and Asia, and the shield of Europe, whence he expelled the barbarians by his holy arms is the first to be buried in this beloved city, whose Founder he was."

I explored the city of Valletta, which is still as La Valette built it, ready to withstand a siege at any moment, in a karrozzin, a nice, slow, horse-drawn carriage.

There is nothing really Maltese about a karrozzin, and in fact these coaches are an idea from Sicily, which is fairly near Malta. They were introduced as a tourist attraction—someone said they are like horsedrawn four poster beds—but they are a pleasant means of seeing the city, when the sun is hot.

As we jogged peacefully along I noticed the straight streets and the square blocks of buildings—Valletta has all the appearance of an early example of town planning, and is not a town that just grew up haphazard.

Outside the church of St Publius, I saw something which puzzled me. There were rows and rows of strange round stones which from a distance looked like the bases of ancient pillars that have long since been destroyed.

I asked Michael Vella, our guide, to tell me what they were. Michael, a diminutive seventy-year-old Maltese, with the knowledge of a professor and the energy of a twenty-year-old, looked at me quizzically.

"I wonder if you can guess? I'll give you a clue— it's something to do with the Great Siege."

I didn't have any ideas at all.

"I'll tell you what—if you haven't guessed by the time you go home, I'll arrange for a demonstration."

I couldn't for the life of me see how you could "demonstrate" a row of stones, but Michael was good to his word, and one morning the whole crew turned up, to find four brawny workmen with a huge wooden lever waiting for us outside the church.

At a closer look the stones were obviously giant lids of some kind. The men inserted the lever under one of them, and heaved until the stone slowly started to move. It took all their strength to roll it away, and when it was gone, it revealed an echoing black hole.

"Granaries!" said Michael. "You see, La Valette was taking no chances. The people of Malta could have starved to death in that siege. So, when he built all the fortifications, he also made those vast stores for grain, so that if Malta was besieged again we would be able to live for a long time without supplies from the outside world. They used them in the last war, you see, so La Valette was right. As a matter of fact, our people were using these granaries until only a few years ago."

Joyce and Mary Farrugia had asked me to meet them "to do the passiegatta." I didn't have time to ask them what it meant, I was just told to be in the Kingsway at six o'clock, so I asked my karrozzin driver to take me there, but to my surprise he looked doubtfully at his watch.

"Too late," he said. "I take you to the top of Kingsway, but I cannot go further."

I thought at first that it was his knocking-off time, but then I saw the police putting up *No Entry* signs at the beginning of the street. The whole of the Kingsway, a long straight street which runs right through the centre of the city, was closed to traffic, and absolutely packed with pedestrians. I was a little alarmed at first, and quite relieved to find Mary and Joyce waiting for me.

"Is it some kind of demonstration?" I asked. The girls fell about with laughter.

"No—it is just the passiegatta—it happens every night. Come and see for yourself."

There were pedestrian barriers running along the narrow pavement on either side of the street. Leaning along the barriers, with studious expressions like stockmen at a cattle auction, were ranged all the young men of the town. The objects of their attention were the girls of Valletta, in force, arm in arm, giggling furiously, and strolling up and down the length of the street. Some were casting inviting glances, others were playing hard to get, and all of them were dressed to kill. Some of the boys were doing the walking bit as well, but most of them were nonchalantly propping up lamp-posts:

"Standing on the corner
  Watching all the girls go by."

Let no one complain about noise pollution from traffic. The sound of footsteps, whoops, wolf-whistles, conversation and giggles of the assembled youth of Valletta would drown any rush hour I've ever heard! Although it was much more exciting to listen to!

The parade continued for two hours, slowly up to the top of the Kingsway, slowly down again.

At eight o'clock the police remove the *No Entry* signs, the street is handed back to the motor cars, and the promenaders disappear until six o'clock the following night, when it starts all over again.

The Fortress Island Opens its Doors

Valletta was built like a fortress, to stand siege and repel invaders. In Malta, wherever you look, you see great towering walls of golden limestone; some, like the cliffs in the south, are made by nature, elsewhere there are huge man-made walls, with turrets and look-out posts. Even the churches look forbidding, with twin cannon flanking massive doors. Not only Valetta, but the whole island looks like a fortress, built to keep people out.

Today all the siege architecture is outdated, for now Malta welcomes visitors, from wherever they come, for her most highly-prized industry is tourism.

Today Maltese workers are not building fortifications, but great hotels with swimming-pools, where holiday-makers can enjoy themselves on one of the sunniest islands in the Mediterranean.

I loved my stay on Malta; not only was I able to go sightseeing, exploring the fortresses and the churches, but I had time to enjoy the sunshine. I swam idly in the swimming-pool of the hotel where we were all staying, I had a go at water-skiing on the blue Mediterranean water, and I worked hard at achieving a golden tan that would be worthy of the honey island!

The Blue Grotto

All the tourists who land on Malta every year try to go to one curious beauty spot. It is called the Blue Grotto, and it is on the south side of the island.

It can only be visited on calm days, so I was glad

that on the day we had chosen the sea seemed glassy-smooth.

At a little fishing village called Wied-iz-Zurrieq a group of us walked along a narrow jetty, and boarded a small Maltese boat, traditionally used for fishing, but fitted with an outboard motor, and used today for ferrying tourists to see one of the island's marvels.

At first we chugged close to the land, under towering limestone cliffs where gulls and tiny sea-swallows found a precarious resting place. Then we made for an opening, a kind of arched doorway in the cliffs themselves. We were surrounded by a soft darkness, but from the entrance of the cave the strong sun filtered through, lit up the white walls, and was reflected in the shimmering water.

The boatman took his paddle, and dipped it in the water. Immediately the white wood turned blue in the deep pool surrounding our boat. He put in his hand, all his fingers became soft, transparent greeny-blue—real aquamarine, in fact.

Delighted, we tried it too, and we were all fascinated to see our own hands become strange and unfamiliar, with a phosphorescent blue sheen which dissolved in a shower of silver spray as soon as we pulled them clear of the water.

It was too tempting; we all wanted to swim in the blue water. We dropped in carefully—the deep water in the sunless cavern, only lit by reflected light, was much colder than the sunny world outside.

But it was worth the first shock. It was like magic, turning and swimming, looking at our sea-blue iridescent bodies transformed by the waters of the Blue Grotto.

Too soon, the boatman told us we must go back—
there is a constant queue of sightseers back on the
jetty, waiting to take their turn in visiting the mysterious
cave.

All this time, the Blue Peter cameras had been
turning. That night the film was sent back to technicians in London to be examined.

"Very worried," they signalled out to us, "there is
a blue haze all through the swimming sequence."

We were very relieved to hear it!

St Paul's Shipwreck

The Maltese people have always been renowned for
treating friendly visitors well. Nearly two thousand
years ago, a very famous visitor was washed up on their
shores—he was to be known as St Paul.

Paul of Tarsus became a Christian three years after
the death of Jesus, and he preached the Faith for twenty
years. At last he was arrested in Jerusalem, accused of
teaching rebellion and causing unrest in the Roman
Empire.

Paul was a Roman citizen, and he insisted that he
could be tried by no one but the Roman Emperor
himself. With his friend Luke, he began the long journey
by sea from Jerusalem to Rome. It was autumn, and
bad weather was expected, but the captain of the ship
was anxious to press on, to deliver his cargo and hand
over the prisoners, with their armed escort.

Paul protested: "I tell you, if you do not put into
port, you will risk losing this ship and every soul
aboard." But the captain insisted on putting to sea.

Before long they ran into a terrible storm, with a

81

fierce north-easterly wind. The crew and passengers were terrified, thinking they would all be drowned.

Paul said to them: "It's a pity you didn't take my advice, but God has heard my prayers, and told me that we shall all get safe ashore."

The ship ran aground, and the sailors and prisoners scrambled through the breakers, and managed to get to shore.

Today there is a huge statue overlooking the strip of coast where St Paul's ship ran aground; for nearly two thousand years it has been known to the people of Malta as St Paul's Bay. We know about the incident because Paul's friend Luke wrote an account of it, which is in the Bible: "Once we made our way to safety we identified the island as Malta. The rough islanders treated us with uncommon kindness. Because it was cold they lit a bonfire, and made us all welcome."

Tradition says that Paul gathered sticks for the bonfire, but he was very short-sighted, and one of the sticks he grabbed turned out to be a poisonous snake. Paul just shook the snake off calmly, it never even bit him, and the islanders started thinking he must have some special powers.

While they were waiting for a new ship, Paul and Luke were taken to the house of Publius, the Roman Governor of Malta. His father had been taken ill, and was dying of fever, but Paul and Luke were able to cure him. Publius was so grateful that he asked them both to stay at his villa, but they wanted to go somewhere quiet, where they could work and pray.

They moved to a cave, in the centre of the island, and lived there for three months. Today a great church has been built over it, but the cave has been preserved just as it was. Here Paul prayed and talked and preached to the people of Malta, and converted the islanders to the Christian faith they follow so enthusiastically to the present day. One of the first to be converted was Publius, and Paul made him the leader of the Church in Malta—its first Bishop.

Another church now stands on the very place where Publius had his home, and it is dedicated to St Paul.

Eventually, when the spring came, another ship appeared, so Paul had to leave the island where he had found such kindness and continue his journey to Rome. There he was tried, and put to death, for being a Christian.

He is remembered by the people of Malta as their own Apostle, who first brought them the Christian faith that for centuries has been an important part of their lives.

St Paul's Day in Rabat

A town called Rabat has grown up around the cave where Paul and Luke stayed, and Rabat celebrates St Paul's day each year with boisterous enthusiasm.

Every village festival has its speciality, and Rabat's speciality is horse racing! Not horse racing like they have at Ascot or Newmarket—the course runs on a road outside the town, and some of the horses are mules, and others are donkeys.

The races were scheduled to start at five-thirty, but nothing happened until about six, which is not an uncommon occurrence in Malta. No one takes the races terribly seriously, it's all part of the fun, and the Maltese have a great talent for enjoying themselves.

The spectators sat on dry-stone walls, drinking hot cokes, chewing very chewy sweets, waiting for someone to shout: "They're off!" This, as far as the first race was concerned, was easier said than done.

It was a donkey race, and after much pushing, shoving and "whoaing", the contestants were roughly lined up for the start. However, on the command "Go", only three donkeys passed the starting line heading for the finish, some passed the line heading for the left-hand wall, not a few failed to pass the starting line at all.

Start number two was slowly organised but this time none of them moved towards the finish; one made a bee-line for the left-hand wall again, possibly to examine an interesting looking hole he'd spotted the first time, and into which he now stuck his head. One or two pulled their riders round in ever-decreasing circles, most didn't even do that.

Eventually at the fourth attempt (or was it the fifth?) and with the aid of a firecracker, the whole line shot off at great speed, mostly in confusion, but anyway heading for the finish.

The crowd went mad, and leapt off the wall, waving their arms and cheering as the flashing legs disappeared into a cloud of dust.

Race number one was finally under way!

The Festival at Siggiewi Gets Under Way

Meanwhile, back in Siggiewi, things were hotting up in the preparations for St Nicholas.

Mr Farrugia, when he wasn't practising the althorn, was busy cutting out and glueing flags to decorate the balcony. The Friday of the festival turned out to be the

Farrugias' twentieth wedding anniversary, providing a double celebration. That evening Mr Farrugia produced an enormous and beautifully iced cake, which was absolutely delicious, as all the crew can testify! Just something Mr Farrugia had knocked up quickly between blowing his horn and making his flags!

He let me help him on one of the flag-making sessions, which I thoroughly enjoyed. It was very nice to have someone showing *me* how to fold the paper and where to put the glue!

Friday night was the first of the band recitals, which was to take place in the square at ten o'clock. After playing there for an hour, they were due to march down the main street, right past the Farrugias' house. In the morning Mr Farrugia and Nicholas were out in the square putting up flags, and helping to erect the bandstand. The church already had its festival awnings hung, and villagers were busy decorating the outside with fairy lights and garlands of ivy. By this time ivy and fairy lights had been added to the paper flags outside the Farrugia balcony.

At eight in the morning, and mid-day, fireworks that sounded like the Third Siege of Malta were let off in deafening bangs. Of course, this wasn't the big display —just part of the practice run-ups that had been going on every day for the past week.

At half-past nine in the evening, we all waved Mr Farrugia off to the recital. All the girls had put on their "Friday" dresses, and I wore something I hoped would be suitable. Mrs Farrugia said "That's a pretty dress, Val," so I thought I must have got it right.

I suggested that it was time we went up to the balcony, as the band was due to march past any moment. "You need not hurry, Val," said Mary. "They'll not be here for hours yet—and you'll know in plenty of time."

About an hour and a half later we picked up the distant sound of a brass band, accompanied by shouts, cheers, explosions, whistles, yells, screams and a pall of black smoke. We took our places up on the balcony, armed with crates of paper confetti which we hurled down into the mêlée below. As the smoke cleared, it revealed a group of whirling, dancing men. They grabbed a small figure whom I later recognised as the bandmaster, and hoisted him shoulder high, and danced while he lurched precariously from one side of the street to the other.

Then the band hove into sight, playing staunchly by the light of lanterns carried by a troupe of boys.

A small statue of St Nicholas followed the band, and the ladies of Siggiewi followed that.

The procession continued to weave its way round Siggiewi for the next two hours. And that was only the first day of the festival!

The Oracle Speaks

The inhabitants of Malta have long been religious; five thousand years ago, before Christianity came to the island, the primitive people followed a pagan fertility cult. They worshipped the goddess Mother of the earth, who, they believed, caused the crops to grow, the trees and vines to bear fruit, and the flocks and herds to have young.

There are many temples of the fertility cult still to be seen in Malta, and they are certainly among the oldest buildings in the world today.

Our guide Michael Vella, who knows and loves every corner of his native island, was eager to show me all its ancient treasures.

Michael told me that he was going to take me to a prehistoric temple which dated from 2,400 BC, so I was rather surprised when our car stopped in the middle of a village street, and he led the way into what looked like a very ordinary house. The temple, he told me, was discovered by accident in 1902, when the owners of the house were digging a well. Suddenly the earth fell away, and they stepped into a chamber that had not been entered for more than four thousand years.

It was still eerie and damp and dark, and extremely cold after the burning Maltese sun outside.

Michael pointed out some strange hollows scooped out of the rock.

"This is where the devil-worshippers would come to sleep and dream their dreams," he said. "Then when they woke they would go to the oracle to have it interpreted."

"Where was that?" I asked.

"Follow me," said Michael, and we went down another flight of stone steps until we came to a clearing with a semicircle of stone seats.

"Here they would tell their dreams to the priest," Michael explained. "Then he would leave them here, while he went to consult the oracle. Now—imagine you have just had your dream, and told it to me—I am the priest. It's very dark and ghostly and strange, and you are alone. Please stay where you are."

He suddenly disappeared behind a shoulder of rock, I could hear his footsteps echoing through the chamber. Then, silence—just the slow drip-drip of water from the roof away in the distance.

"Michael?" I called softly.

No reply.

"Michael?" I tried a little louder. This time I just heard my own voice boom back. Then silence again.

Then came a booming sound, which started to get louder and louder, until the whole chamber was filled with an awful, deep pulsating voice.

"I am the oracle—I am the oracle," thundered over and over again.

To my intense relief, Michael bobbed up again from behind the rock, his brown puckish face creased in smiles.

"Did you hear it?" he asked. "Isn't it fantastic? Come, and I'll show you how it is done."

He took me down some narrow stairs to a small hole in the rock.

"Now listen," he commanded. He stood on tip-toe, and put his face to the hole. Again the rock chamber was filled with the ghostly voice, which seemed to come, not from Michael, but from everywhere else—it was all around us.

He stepped back from the hole.

"Now you do it," he instructed me.

I did exactly as Michael had done: I stood in exactly the same place, and made a low moaning sound in exactly the same way.

And nothing happened. It just sounded like me making a silly, low moaning noise.

"You see," said Michael, delightedly, "it never works for a woman—only a man's deep vocal chords will make it work."

I tried once again, but it was no good.

"I don't think that's fair," I complained.

Michael smiled his razor smile.

"Well, you see, Valerie, the oracle had never heard of Women's Lib."

Fireworks on Saturday

Fireworks are one of the great features of all the Maltese festivals. They range from the most massive bangers in the world, to the most magnificent and ingenious pyrotechnic displays I have ever seen.

The bangers are called petards, and they consist of a circular fuse with about half a dozen charges which go off in rotation, like a burst of rapid fire from an automatic rifle, only louder. Every 8 September they celebrate the end of the Great Siege by letting off hundreds of petards—a strange way to celebrate their relief from continual bombardment! Most of these fireworks are home-made, and every year there are casualties—some, I hate to say, are fatal—among the firework makers who haven't got it quite right.

However, I'm happy to say that the Saturday night Siggiewi firework display went off without a hitch.

It started with some spectacular rockets, sent off from a field below Siggiewi. From our camera position outside the village we had a commanding view, as the mushrooming spray of rockets soared up and over the fairy lights of the church, picking out the façade and the dome with little jiggling pinpoints of light.

Later on, the display in the square started, one man's work for a year going up in smoke in forty-five minutes. But it was magnificent while it lasted, with huge geometric shapes, and bicycles with rotating wheels, ridden by cyclists whose legs pumped up and down. Then a firework aeroplane took off, and flew low over the heads of the crowd, towed on an invisible wire.

The finale was a display of rockets which seemed to arrive from outer space, before they exploded in a million coloured stars about the church of St Nicholas.

Nicholas Mangion, the creator of the display, wiped a tear from his eye, whether from emotion or the cordite fumes it was difficult to say. Flushed with success, he received the warm congratulations of the crowd before he went off home to bed.

Tomorrow he would start work again—for St Nicholas day, 1975.

Sunday of the Festival

Sunday is the climax of the Siggiewi festival, and has a much less frenetic atmosphere. It begins with High Mass in St Nicholas' Church, and after the Mass an enormous statue of St Nicholas is solemnly processed through the streets.

I joined Mrs Farrugia, young Nicholas, Joyce, Mary and Rita for the moment the statue appeared at the door of the church. Mr Farrugia was busy with the band, and Beppe was in the procession. An excited murmur spread through the crowd as the great double doors in front of the church slowly swung open. Then a row of men, in long white albs with crimson capes appeared, their shoulders bent under the tremendous weight of the *twenty-foot-high* statue of the patron saint of Siggiewi.

It was a baroque statue on a gold base, showing the

The statue of St Nicholas

saint with a flowing beard and dressed as a bishop, with crozier and mitre. The moment the saint appeared the crowd went wild, cheering and clapping their hands. There was a cannonade of fireworks, and vast blizzards of confetti were flung from the top of the church doorway. It was a very un-English occasion, and I felt as I often have done when attending Mediterranean religious festivals, slightly shocked by the extravagance of it all, yet genuinely moved by the infectious enthusiasm of the people.

The great statue slowly wobbled its way down the steep flight of steps. I felt quite alarmed because the bearers were all elderly men; the honour of carrying the statue is jealously guarded, and handed down from father to son. At one moment there was a gasp of fright from the crowd as the statue lurched to one side, but miraculously (with doubtless many a muttered prayer to St Nicholas) the old men recovered their balance and St Nicholas regained his equilibrium.

Mrs Farrugia looked suitably weepy as Beppe in his beautifully ironed white cotta filed solemnly past, carrying his tall yellow candle. Every so often the procession stopped and St Nicholas was rested on carved golden supports while the bearers recovered their breath.

It took at least three hours to troop the massive statue round the square, but the enthusiasm of the people of Siggiewi didn't flag for an instant.

The Maltese people live a simple and, some might say, primitive life compared with most Europeans, but they seem to have something which many of us who lead more sophisticated lives have lost. There is a knack of living as a community, and of all working together with enthusiasm for something that really matters to every individual in the village.

I enjoyed my stay on the honey-coloured island, and I was grateful to the Maltese, particularly the people of Siggiewi, and above all to the Farrugia family, for allowing me, for ten short days, to become a member of their community, and a patriot for the festival of Siggiewi.

In the same series:
Blue Peter Special Assignment
Isle of Skye, Isle of Wight and Isle of Man

Come with Val to three islands off the coast of Britain. First to trace the steps of Bonnie Prince Charlie to the misty Isle of Skye, and visit a school where bagpipes and Gaelic are on the timetable. Second to the Isle of Man— to uncover the strange story of the Snaefell mine disaster, to find out how kippers are made, and to ride round the famous TT racecourse on a moped! Third to the Isle of Wight, the holiday island discovered by the Romans. A "perfect little paradise" Queen Victoria called it. Val tries out her bathing machine, and the Blue Peter film crew gets marooned on a lighthouse.